KHOI

KHOI

by

JOHN HENDRICKSE

New Beacon Books
London. Port of Spain

First published 1990
by New Beacon Books Ltd.,
76 Stroud Green Road, London N4 3EN, England

© 1990 John Hendrickse

ISBN: 0901241 96 2 hardback
       0901241 97 0 paperback

Printed by Villiers Publications Ltd.,
26a Shepherds Hill, London N6 5AH, England

PREFACE

As a young boy I sat in an overcrowded, noisy and badly equipped classroom, listening to a teacher telling us that, "in 1713 all the Khoi were wiped out in a smallpox epidemic." We the children of Khoi ancestry sat there listening to a fabricated history that told us we did not exist. The people of the Cape with their signs, their gestures, their voices were told that they had no voice. That thoughts had to be constructed through the action of the oppressor if we were to survive.

But what happens when the word is not of the body's action: but imposed on a body whose language has been obliterated by oppression. It is in this theatre of carnage that I address my readers. Trying to oppose a language through which we act and name, and are named. I reflect myself through a language that has deflected me. Thought struggles to find the body and the body struggles to find expression. In the poem EVA the words speak for themselves:

"Only then can you understand
What it is like to be invaded by words
that do not cling or sing
with the drumming heartbeat of the body"

It is through thought not words that the imagination affirms that the body exists. But words, action, thought, imagination, and time together will create an alchemy of words; manifesting a new body of culture. The rolling mist that has blocked our vision will evaporate, watering new words that will grow in meaning. I therefore make no apology for not using standard English. Allow the words to move your body and filter into the brain to take their position in relation to meaning; mantric meaning that will haunt the imagination.

They say in poetry the individual's breathing determines the length and shape of line. That the body's action determines the syntax. But not to see beyond the body, is not to see the body. We have measured our success through how close we could imitate our masters. But now it is important that we pay homage to the failures of our culture, for it is they who have left us our legacy.

Never mind

Never mind hey!

ere's more than enough
to go around
but people must mos
march and shout
and riot for a diet

KHOI

TO TINA

Whose help I really appreciated
and Jan and Carl who brought my ego down to earth

MEETING

IN THE BEGINNING

Oananua . . . .
Created
in the origins of suffering
From
the formless inchoate mass

CREATED
in a time
when Kanya God of fire
in the heat of passion
brought you into being

In the ceremony of birth
devoid of tenderness
you met the exploding peak
hissing its desires
the hot lava of glowing arteries
demanded your submission

Away from the heat of consummation
away from the heat of burning desire

In search of bodily comfort

With the stealth of the future
and the cunning of the Khoi
you escape from the
Sacred Mountains of the Amatolas

Away from the heat into
the articulate cool soft air

Where valediction in a dream
green dream green
bathed in translucent light
came into being

Meeting the figure
of a giant Mantis
weaving a spiral
in the dance of the spirit

Splendid in the dream dance
Entwined with the earth and sky

Oananua

In the universe of dreams
in the creation of love

You could not resist the
gentle touch and gentle eyes of Mantis

Your yellow body glowed towards
the unity of green
in the beadwork of reality and myth
and wrapped in dreams you created Khoi

But Kanya
mad with jealousy
mad with hate
hissing with heat

Sought – you – found – you
and killed you

Mantis mourned your death
then his dance of creation
became the dance of destruction

Bathed in red blood
of a fluorescent sunset
he danced the darkness
of a new dance before the sunrise

The vision of dawn the crack of day
The vision of death the crack of Mantis
an orgasm of death exploding
making the earth quake with terror

Mantis roared with the breath of destruction
hurricaned in it's fury it killed the flames
of Kanya

Flames that could not burn exploded
bursting Kanya wide open

Form broke, reformed and broke again

In the silence of nothing Kanya disappeared

The dream of Mantis – the green dream green
grew into the grass upon the ground
While Mantis weaves the spiral dance
amongst the plants and minds of KHOI

THE WHITE PLAGUE

Three white shrouds
walked upon the water

coming nearer and nearer
in our direction

their white chested sails
billowing in the wind

Our shouts echoed
across the flat topped mountain

which stood hard against the earth
blue against the sky
yet brown under our feet

This Omen
this cloud of dreams
kept floating towards us

we left the beach
standing on top of Table Mountain

we saw the ships unveil themselves
the Reiger – the Goede Hoop
the Dromedaris

the white dream disappeared
as the shroud was rolled away
skeletons of death pointing to the sky

fire and water had come together
earth and air stood watching
waiting . . . . to be consumed

We Khoi Khoi
people of the earth
breathed . . . .
and clicked our tongues

unaware of time of clocks
that ticked away our lives

PART 2

We stood in the shadow of Table Mountain
listening to
the creaking ships the screeching gulls

warning us of a vision embedded in violence

This dream of men without feet
leaving footprints too strange to follow

This nightmare this whitemare
the reoccurring nightmare
had once again come back

They had cut a path through the water
a path through which many white dreams
of wealth would pass

Their dreams were our destruction
they spoke with thunder spitting fire
the sound they made was the sound of death

These men of greed defiled the earth
their ears did not hear the
piercing screams of our protected species

Their imagination projected dreams of need
we were in their way – there was no escape

PART 3

Our dreams were dreams of hate
for the white knight
who killed our dreams of black

A dead insect flattened by his boot
Mantis where are you ?

The whitemare has become a reality

Now the fire of hate burned in our souls
we despised our gods for deserting us
we despised ourselves for being humble
we walked in the shadow of our enemy
a crumpled culture hating itself

We had lost the click tongue
taken on a new god – the god of the whiteman

'Bid maar kinders bid maar
dis God se kruis wat ons moes dra'
Gods cross yes gods cross
carried by the Khoi Khoi
carried by the people of the earth

For we prayed for white and lost
ourselves in another man's religion

PART 4

Nothing was straightforward nothing clear
we had become the multi sided man
the man of many angles the anglepoise man
bending our backs for the master race

Our gods had deserted us left us to learn

Haikona haikona

No way no way to go as we walked and walked
to the rhythm of time
and talked and talked to rhythms of white

Then our words became whispers as we talked
and talked in the rhythm of night
to the sound of a new black dream
For we moved again
to the click to the click
To the click of the tongue of the Xhosa sound

EVA

The interpretress, who married Pieter van
Meerhoff a ship's surgeon and explorer, and
ended her days in squalor and drunken disgrace.

You must be born on the junction of desolation
allowing white words to occupy your soul
Only then can you understand
what it is like to be invaded by words
that do not cling or sing
with the drumming heartbeat of the body

In your drunken delirium
you must hear the echo of your soul
making the proclamation of your people
and listen to the wind whisper to the earth

HEY MALAU MALAU WAKE UP

Time and time – many times ago has blurred
your past and lick your mother tongue
from your lips

Everything was moving up and down
like a merry-go-round one false step
and you could fall on the face of agony

In the cold light of survival
You watched time pass
domesticated in the life
of a ship surgeon's wife

But his accurate eye watching
the twang of the bow string
his swift and agile movements
how would you avenge your father's death

You tried to suckle the breast of your
mothers culture, only to be met with rejection
the poison arrow was turned towards you

Fantasies now dissolved into falsities
wearing your starched white kappie
you watched your people
as they watched you with suspicion
To them you were one of those
to those you were one them

Drinking the wine but not eating the bread
because the flesh was tainted, hunger made you
die a million times

In garbled words you were heard to say
MAJIETAS,MAJIETAS,
JULLE KAN MY NIE VOESTAAN NIE

CORNELIUS

A Khoi was sent to England
for education, but when he returned they
regretted that they had sent him. He
became one of the many revolutionaries

He came from the upper world and saw
existence paled by sun starvation
tempting him to meet extinction
only his dreams shortened the distance of home

Here was no warmth or friendship
Calculating eyes only watched his agony

Actually talks
Actually eats
A witness – bearer of their exploration

Authenticated as genuine primitive
for the hollow eyes of industry

Pricked by the thorns of civilisation
He was taught how to talk
how to dress, how to dance
somersaulting, cartwheeling
and standing on his hands,
but he did not do the minuet

The devils eyes danced with
a beckoning glance

tempting him to become the in-between
the go-between,
a screaming man who lost his soul

This was a man planned land
the Hell they talked about
This place was white on black
a negative of his home

They killed the ground
with hard cold stone
how could he dance, when his feet
could not feel the soil

Where were the animals?
trapped like people
in cages – or harnessed to work

With silent thoughts
his ancient mind waits for a sign of freedom
He knew their future was his destruction

UNCERTIFIED BIRTHRIGHT

Cutting down their heritage
they raked away the weeds
under the name of civilisation
they planted new words foreign to an old people

While under mind arrest
white surveillance watched
feeding them with infected words

Grotesquely they grunted the sounds
fugitive words fled from their minds
contaminated with the sound of imprisonment
they opened their mouths – only to converse
with a muzzle of a musket

They asked for water and were given words
with the stench of death still in their nostrils
and the stench of suffering still in the air

Dazed they gulped down the words
a necessity for their survival
and they mumbled back the vomit
bitter bitter words of gall
that could not be digested

Words that told them
they were non-people, and labelled them inferior
words that called them
Cape Coloured, Hotnot, and primitive

Now the arrows are tipped
with the poison of your words
the bows are tight ready to snap
under the strain of your suppression

The arrows are your words returning

BUT

Will the villainy you teach be executed
and shall it go hard with you
or will they better the instruction ?

JUDASES

The inner darkness of remembrances
the exotic white face
selling beads tobacco and illusions
they gave them a cap to hold in their hands
and named them KAPITAANS

Their minds mountaineered
high into the distant sky
away from the earth dancing in the sky
suspended by their dreams

In a history of betrayal, and denial
the emaciated mind
provoked by temptation starved of
recognition, accepted the

Judas words they had to say

Now trembling with cap in hand
the Kapilaans plead for power

While the people pay with their lives
lamenting as they bury their dead
under tombstones in a racist cemetery

HYENA

With eyes peering
into the darkness

He laughs – Hungry for death

There is no need for graves
the victims disappear
in the muffled shadows of the night

He stumps along on bumble knees
with his big back rump protruding

The nape of his bulging neck
has a shag of hair
caked in his victims blood

Snatching his share of the kill
the razor sharp teeth
cuts down the vision of tender youth
mother of birth sees the maker of death

BUTCHER

You have pulled away the meat
that once was my child
leaving a dismembered carcass

WE KNOW YOU

Oh yes we know you
by the smell of death

MALAU

JOKER IN THE WHITE PACK

At night alone on the stoep
huddled in his own arms
The dreaming body of a boy
sleeps with the myth of motherhood
Away from the violence
Away from the raw cuts and words
that bulldozed through his brain
that placed him in a position
of grateful subservience

Words that named him BOOI-BOSIE-HOTNOT
But his official title was HOUSE BOY

Now he needed sleep to touch his mother
that mother who they said had abandoned him

He was told how the Misses heart was moved
by the pitiful cries of a black baby
Found in a bush wrapped in newspaper
wrapped in words of a whiteman's tongue

LIES ALL LIES – he knew for certain
he'd been stolen from his parents

They demanded gratitude he could not give
Their pity conferred on him an obligation
a curse of fate that was worse than death
his body taut under the white Misses touch
made her tenderness turn to violence

One day his father will find him
his mothers touch will soothe
the throbbing
sobbing brain and take away the pain

But the unforeseen lies in the forest
of knowledge waiting to attach itself
In school the fool (the wind uprooted tree)
bowed by the innocent shattered by the truth
Was told about the secrets of the white guilt
and he was forced to recognise himself

His black face looked at the mirror
and he saw reflected before him
    HIS GRANDFATHER the boss
    HIS GRANDMOTHER the Misses
    HER DAUGHTER his mother
    HER HUSBAND his father
Those children had killed his father
and he would never be found
He hated them hated truth hated himself
and the Misses Oh how she hated education

REMEMBER

Melodies break, disintegrate
the throbbing silence is obliterated

Fingers move picking through the density of sound
struggling to give form to chaos

White ears trying to wash away the guilt
allowing sound to lash them into submission

Delicious sweet lyrical phrases tender pain
touching love but sharp as it splits
through sound making mythology from
ghosted dreams breaking the apartheid mind

Fingers crisscross the keys, faster and faster
scream sounds whip the audience demanding
Raging against the jarring sounds
tearing through the music

HEY KAFFIR

Where did you steal that culture
Where did you steal that suit
Fear gave him that sinking feeling
he'd been stealing dignity

His fingers minuet the music
anger rises up inside of him
the warrior walks through the white menace
the music stumbles in staccato phrases

Hey Kaffir se Bass
Hey Kaffir se Bass
Blerry Kaffir
walking around
as bold as brass

The music crashes staggering along the keyboard
groping as he is kneed in the groin
the rolling bass hand continues
no tune as he rolls over in pain
Vicious sharp cutting sounds reflect their voices
thudding boots bury deep into his flesh

Triumphant and free but in agony big sounds echoed
the bleeding broken man who tried to stand with

DIGNITY
Sounds race across the keyboard zig-zagging
through violence, for he wouldn't die for dignity

The music forces itself forward into freedom
the white menace hanging onto his jacket

The sound rips through the air
as the jacket is torn from his shoulders

Free from the new jacket
free from APARTHEID hate hate
free from the fascist who shout

KILL THE FOKEN KAFFIR

His finger fly nimbly across the keys
the ground flying beneath his feet

THE MUSIC STOPS

Then starts with big sounds of the revolution
playing the anthem NKOSI SIKELEL'I AFRICA

Becoming louder and louder ending on a Crescendo

THE UNMENTIONED MARTYRS

Unable
to sit at the table of her parents
and talk

Unable
in my misery to mourn her death

Unable
to follow in single file
the slow black silence
of a memory mourned

Unable
to shout my anger to awaken apathy
to stand and pronounce
the murder most foul
of love unable to flourish

I Khoi Khoi men of men
accepted black was bad
that
it was the embodiment
of all carnal desire

The desire of flesh sex and hell
thrilled me

Damnation was all part
of my CRUCIFIXION

I was going to purge myself
of abuse through sex

WE MET
She feeling guilty
I angry as hell
at being the product of abuse

She understood my anger
understood my isolation
my fight for recognition

WE were alone in a society
sick with hate
sick with fear

She felt my body tremble
as she touched me

I was afraid that truth would
thunder its voice against
UNJUST LAWS and make me a martyr
of a just cause

I was not prepared to fight
I needed no man to say

BEWARE THE IDES OF MARCH

Yet self destruction drove us on
We were drawn to the edge
of a precipice and there was nothing

WE COULD DO

We made love with danger
entering the realms
of fear and delight
opening the dam below the soft mound
allowing the river of pleasure
to flow freely

But making love in secret
making love with guilt
making love with shame
was our problem

ASHAMED
of being gaoled
ashamed
of being outcasts
ashamed
of being found out

DROVE US TO DISASTER
ENDING IN DEATH

Death of our child
who never had a chance

Death of a mother
not daring to face the world

and I like her
with fear of being found out
cried silently

Cried without a tear

INVISIBLE MAN

Alone
as I walked along the beach

Away from Hyena City
scavengers of Europe

Away from the roar of traffic
fast food and quick death

Away from the wind
that blows through dusty streets

unsettling the dirt
that was always there

moving it along
into crevasses the eye cannot see

But it is from dirt
that big trees grow
that big buildings are built

Dirt and labour
make nice homes
nice cared for gardens
for nice respectable people

How do I get away from the
planned consciousness of the Cape
built round a fort
built from a consciousness of fear

I walked along the beach
the sea was warm and the wind was wild
obliterating all footsteps
while it spewed it debris on the
WHITE SEA SAND

I lay down
my eyes fixed on the rolling clouds

I pictured my blood as it oozed
out of my body
seeping into the sand mingling with
the foam

I needed to become at one with
the sea and the sand

But red blood left a stain
a dark red stain on the white sea sand

This was my guilt

The sea did what it did
it was itself it was the sea

It would wash the sand clean
not because of want
This was the way of the sea

I did what I should do to survive
but this was not me

I was a picture of what I should be
in a white man's reality

DIVIDED TRAIN

Standing on a platform
inviting new invaders
to death with me

waiting to get on
and glide forward into
a new reality

waiting for a train
under surveillance
of new events

Standing on the station
square slabs of concrete

Division between line
and platform

signs of civilisation
signs slam against the eyes
WHITES ONLY – SLEGS VIR BLANKES

Signs of division

Forced to stand where goods
are loaded onto the train
at the end of the station
near the dead flesh of the cadavers
Springboks necks twisted awkwardly
eyes wide with surprise

A sacred symbol of our people
taken by the rugger bugger
murdered by the hunt

Soft gentle eyes stare into nothingness
Shot in the leap of life

God has the gun aimed at me
to kill the devil inside of you

Signs of civilisation

Coal dust – Asbestos dust – Gold dust
Their profits
All part of our death

ALL SIGNS OF CIVILISATION

MEDICINE MAN

He touched me
old man on his haunches

Wild bush hair and white cotton beard,
glow-worm eyes headlighting
the cracked bracken face and earth forehead.

Hands of branches beckoned me,
the rustling voice repeating.

"Yet as I die yet dying live
in the minds of my ancestral future."

I scratch my memory, the dry psyche
of a cold white consciousness.
He scratches marks on the soft dry sand,
the sun creeps through the green foliage

it creeps into my soul;
Heitsi-Eibib father of the hunt,
I have found the ancestral past with
those shadowy long-forgotten ghosts:

They haunt my frightened mind,
and the gulf is wide and splits reality;
but the Hare's message still lingers –

"As I die and dying perish,
I shall die utterly die."

THE PHOENIX

They advise restraint and stealth
but what are our conjugal rights with half
blood brothers and sisters who have abused us
in the name of progress for personal power

For they have stripped us of our birthright
disenfranchised us,
before they blinded us with words
now we are the working dead of progress
mispronounced by the branches of security

They have built houses with our sweat and hunger
They have grown fat and, treachery has helped them
to build this fabricated myth of civilisation

Security branches have built barb-wired walls
keeping in the unwanted keeping out the ignorant
But from those walls of Black detention
and white protection came a voice

The voice of a woman singing about a bird who
remembers its freedom
although trapped in a cage

As she sang I heard the clapping of hands
the stamping of feet the laughter
the flowing river going over the rapids

I saw the crescent moon smile
yellow against the back drop of the dark sky
that nodded and winked at us, as the orchestra of
the night spoke to our unconscious
hypnotic names hynotic sounds choked by the
noise of industry.

We were locked away from the cloudless skies
the green flames of the fields
The rain the sun
the changing seasons were replaced by

UNCHANGING ATTITUDES

Roofs walls and wooden floors were protection
protecting civilisation from nature
from secret desires from soft succulent juices
of fruit after they have been plucked

From the black demon the demon of nature
who allowed his skin to touch the air
who allowed his feet to touch the earth

This demon danced with the thunder of the drums
and his way the will of the wind

I escaped from civilisation towards the demon
only to be trapped in a labyrinth
where fragments of reality exploded into nightmares

    Who was this white phoenix
    who arose from black ashes?

The invisible hand is wielding a bow
the silent arrow is perfumed with poison
the phoenix fall from the sky

THERE IS A SHRIEK AS REALITY IS REVIEWED

Its existence was only echoed in their dreams

CHAMELEON

There is no bridge
between the banks of a river
between the flowing waters of freedom

You have clawed at the door
knocking yourself out
demanding entrance

The sign above reads
WHITES ONLY

Chameleons can change colour
but changing colour
does not remove pain and hunger

You are invisible but food
for thought creates the movement

The rolling eyes
the flick of the long tongue
has made you vulnerable

You writhe
under the cold-eyed glances
of the blue-eyed predators

You search in darkness
to hide your white deceit
Whispers behind white entrances
not really – not one of us

You try to duck
words thrown in both directions
you own words are like jokes
in an empty hall

They extract your mind
there is no pain killer
only the constant drill
making a hole in your head

You have eaten white bait
There is a hole in your head
they have hooked away your mind

The changing colour
bulging rolling eyes
the flick of the long tongue
all reflex movements

Unlike the leopard the Chameleon
always changes his spots

MARIE JOHANNA DREAM
(Marijuana)

My metal mind
kisses Marie Johanna
Two trains of thought
trapped in a railway siding
clang together

Waves thunder through my head
dripping water ooze through eyes
tears of my own betrayal
for the gift of becoming

Soft sand cradles the body
caressed by oblivion
man in the dance of betrayal
with the head of a Hyena

Kiss my lips and draw me close
for we did meet and I did see
AUTSHUMOA the man himself

They called him Herry
Herry the Hotnot
Swaying to himself he tries to catch
the rhythm of the waves

His voice calls TUSUI XGOA
The father of all fathers
his eyes peer into the space beyond
fading through the cobwebs of history
he disappears but his chant lingers in my mind

"He come he come to meet me
man with far reaching thoughts
follow my thoughts
he come he come to meet me"

We dance the dance of betrayal
the ultimate dance of death
I kissed the last of Marie Johanna
and killed it in the soft wet sand

BRA JONAS

TJANKGELUID

Wie het op my kop geklop – Wie het op my siel gestaan
Wie het my oë toegesluit en die doekies omgedraai

EK KAN DIT NIE VERSTAAN NIE

Wie het my dronkgeslaan
en my lewe gesteel met leë beloftes
Wie het my naamloos gemaak en vreemde woorde
af in my keel gesteek
Wie staan met bebloede hande agter sy rug
en 'n glimlag op sy gesig

Daar is oorsak en gevolg
Die onderste speek kom ook bo

Bewusteloos loop ek deur die geklop
mal met haat klap ek die windmeul – die wind skree
maar niemand luister – ek gesels met die dodeland mure
is donkergrys die lug is bloodrooi
Ons leef van hand tot tand

Hoe kan ek beskryf die kletter van die eind
Grafte grooi met kruise, daar is geen nuus om jou
te vertel maar ons weet ons sal nie vergeet nie

Maak die gordyne oop en kyk hoe die lug van die
ondergaande son stroom oor die land
Die goggatjies flits heen en weer gulsig-
uitgevreet Trots dat hulle kan bo ons koppe vlieg

MAAR PAS OP jy sal nie altyd ons bloed suip nie
Daar staan jy met vroom bakkies asof botter nooit
in jou mond sal smelt nie

Maar jy knyp die kat in die donker jy klop op ons
deur in die nag en in die môre met bebloede hande
glimlag jy

EK KAN DIT NIE VERSTAAN NIE

Daar is geen lug maar die son skyn
Hierdie woorde is misleidend daar is lug in die verte en
elke rantjie is gevlek met bloedrooi blommetjies

Voeltjies sing in die bossies van vryheid
Die son stroom goud en die bome skyn groen

Daar is geen goggatjies wat oor ons koppe vlieg
Hulle het verdwyn in die geheim van vryheid

En elke rantjie is gevlek met bloederige blommetjies

SOBBINGSOUNDS

Who was knocking in my head –
Who was standing on my soul
Who closed my eyes before they cheated me

I CANNOT UNDERSTAND THIS

Who beat me up – then stole my life with empty
promises – Who took away my name and shoved
strange words right down my throat Who stands
bloody hands behind his back and a broad smile on
his face

There is cause and effect the lowest will also have
his moment on high

Bewildered I walk through the knocks
Mad with hate I attack the windmill the wind screams but
no one listens
I am talking to the dead lands – Walls are dark grey
The sky is blood red – We live from hand to mouth
How can I describe the clatter of the end

Graves grow with crosses there is no news to tell you
But we know and will not forget

Open the curtains and look at the light of the sinking sun
as it floods all over the land

The insects flit around greedy and over fed – proud that
they can fly over our heads

BUT BEWARE you will not always suck our blood

There you stand with that innocent face as if butter would
not melt in your mouth – But the thief in the night knocks
at our door and in the morning – with bloodstained hands
behind your back you smile

I CANNOT UNDERSTAND THIS

There is no light in the land although the sun does shine
These words are misleading in the distant there's light
and every hill is speckled with blood red flowers

The birds sing in the bushes – this is their freedom song
The sun spreads its golden hue and the trees glint green

No insects fly overhead they have disappeared with the
dream of freedom – while every hill is bespattered with
bloodstained flowers

GO DOWN DERE

If you go
If you go
If you go down dere
you'll been gunned down dead
If you go down dere my child

But who ran through the streets
holding a brick
like other children hold a ball
The step child of the western world
awaking to a new Afrika

Parents hear the requiem of revolution
sung by their children and they are afraid

CHILD why don't you listen to me
if you go down dere
they will be there
making guarra guarra wid de guns

They'll take you break you
break you beat you ill treat you

Cause why?
cause you black en dats a fact

BUT MUMMA DARRAH you tell for me
why dey do dis ting
tell for me when dis problem begin?
say to me why
say to me why
cause it hurts me to hear you cry

Child we tried to survive as best we could
worked hard to make a home for you
if you go down dere
you'll be gunned down dead
you'll destroy yourself for dis idea of freedom

They were the birds flying high flying free
Spreading their wings they arose
from the street enclosed city of deprivation
going down there with their fist in the air
fighting against oppression

SEE MUMMA SEE WHAT WE DONE

Ja my child now I bandage up your bleeding wounds
can you not feel my tears as I touch your broken flesh

But Mumma how do you bandage up my bleeding mind
as I watch you quietly shaking your head
your eyes burning wid hate

KUNDALINI

Forked tongue snake
we have reached the parting of the ways
Crushed by the coils of calculation
that has choked our vision
Stifled our reality and poisoned our minds

We have seen you for what you are
and now we bid farewell to fear
weaving and hissing curling in creation
seething for libation of the Deumba dance

In the soft rain of liberation
Wet lips sip the kiss of life
whose wife was husband to the earth
now dance the dance of the Deumba dance

Burrow deep deep down into the sounds
of the hollow brain and hear the cry
moving the body angered by awakening
Angered by recognition that all is not well

The thief of might was scribe to reason
lips whisper words of fear
who searches for contraband intelligence
so we could be taxed for seeing the insanity

Now we dance the Deumba dance of desperation
holding hands with the vanished dream
stamping upon the dust that has blown away
there is no ground in which to bury tradition
it has been concreted by desire and greed

The vapor-trails of an exhausted society
choke us with despair and clouds our vision
civilisation has curled around us squeezing out
dispossessed we dance a Deumba dance

Now we tether our dance and dreams to revolution
We will stamp on the purple pastures of nobility
the unconscious will move the body in seismic waves
and we will rumble with discontent
as we preach the catechism of a new culture

Time to return to peace and contentment
for they too are there to be found in death
nesting above the dream of succession
as we dance the dance of the Deumba dance

A ROAD OF DESTRUCTION
(Death of Bra Jonas's Brother)

Between the shacks
of corrugated iron
and old packing cases

Between the rags
blankets for beds
and boxes for tables

They made a path
a path through human life
with a bulldozer

Between life and death
They made a path of destruction

A clean neat path eradicating
the blood stains of exploitation

They tried to conceal
their guilt by destroying it

But all the perfumes of apartheid
could not hide the smell of oppression

We sat watching waiting
knowing that one day our time will come

This was their time and they
had abused it in the name of progress

Soon we will get the guns
for our protection against this violence

The city turned its face from us
afraid that time was running out

And while it slept
shaking with violent nightmares

The police patrolled
mad with power mad with fear mad with hate

(TRESPASSERS WILL BE PERSECUTED)

A young man black against the night
Sneaks through the forbidden city
His home has been destroyed
destroyed by bulldozers
flattened by progress
flattened by gods chosen people
for the path of righteousness

He darts into a doorway avoiding light
avoiding white avoiding the law

A light shines through the window
his crime of black has been highlighted

He runs for dark his only protection
the gutteral sounds shouts in his ears

He turns in terror to see THE LAW
his feet slap hard against the tarred road

Trying to create a distance between him
and this madness this menacing form

Air burst through his lungs
his heart bangs against his ribs

The silence of the night is broken
a bullet crashes into his back

He slumps into a heap the houses
and lamp poles lay on their sides

He struggles trying to plant his feet
on the earth but the road is tarred and hard

In the distance he hears the explosion of a gun
the ground is knocked from his feet

He falls into the sky the broken strands
of a human being lies at their feet

They kick over the body and look at the face
and look at the face of a young man

With a surprised expression a young face
surprised that death HAD COME SO EARLY

SLAP STICK

Sunday morning
the churchman has pounded my brain
shaken my mind with words

On my bankie
under the Jacarande tree talking
to this joppa from Geranium Street

Waiting for the Sunday meal

Milk of white kindness soured by apartheid
Ney jong
say something better than nothing

But nothing's what we got –
wrapped in nice words
iced with coloured cream and holy water

A pudding for the Sunday meal
mealie meal wrapped in brown skin

while the tongue tastes the saliva
and the mind imagines more

Coloured cream from the milk
of white kindness and the pay is good

But front men get killed in first attack

Sitting on my bankie
under the Jacaranda tree watching
men with cream on their faces
trying to set me free

RECITATION TIME

JOE . . . . .JOE

Jes Sirr??

JOE STAND UP AND SAY YOUR POEM

Er . . . .

COME ON WE HAVE NOT GOT ALL DAY

Morta . . . .er . . . .da Arthur
so all day long
de noise of bettle rolled
until King Arthur
man by man had fallen
er . . . .en . . . .den . . . .

Crap face look at me
wid eyes too narrow to see
got a cane in his hand
dat big teacher man
en he's going to hit de shit out of me

Comfort myself who comforts me?
no fascist like him will set me free

En all day long de noise de noise
of words to put me down

COME ON BOY RECITE YOUR POEM

Dis poem isn't mine
is his lines
to force people like me
to blow dere minds
Wid all de majesty of white mankind

Comfort myself what comfort is dere for me
when teachers stand like gods
but don't know me

Say words say words
all said before
say battle rolled
en all day long en all day long
you battle to bottle up my mind

You tell me to
Say Sir Say Sir say tank you Sir

Ag no! jus hit my hand
you have de cane en dere's my hand
JUS HIT JUS HIT

HANOVER STREET

The removal of sixty thousand mixed race people
from District Six in Central Cape Town
is just one of the many inhuman acts of apartheid

Is all gone now
dose streets where we did hang about

Dose seven steps
where no white man would venture

Dose balconies
wid washing hanging from de line

IS ALL GONE NOW

De law it say
no coloured race mus live in dis location

But Tante Grace did buy her place
en still she had to move

Auntie Grace de modder to us all
use to skell us out

"Ombaskofte layabouts you never pay for noting"

We were fast en easy
down de Strand
Bang de bus
swing de pole
en ho-pe-le we dere

Grab fast
lean back
feet clap
on de road
en go pallie go
cause de bus pull you so

We took what we needed
cause no one wanted to give

BUT NOW DE STREETS ARE EMPTY

No horrible cops
No jew boy shops
No dice game or
Joep from Jakkals Shebeen

It was a no good place
a blerry disgrace
but it was our street

Is all gone now

Dey bulldoze de place
like a bomb hit de buildings

Is all gone now

Years of trouble time gone past
many faces get old fast
many years of sorrow
built into dose buildings

Is all gone now

Dere were happy times too
although dey were few
dey were good times

Tante Grace did pass away
didn't want to make de move
turn her face to de wall en die

But we don't cry cause we got no tears

NOW IS ALL GONE...ALL GONE...GONE
But not forgotten

TROJAN HORSE

Dis is a story of devastation en glory
how kids gave me back my dignity

Jy moes wakker wies
cause sudden death did
hit dis city

It was no holiday
kids didrn't come out to play

No teacher did ring de bell
but out dey came

lighties pickanins
en haregat as hell

I stood on de stoep
wid me bottle a wine

en call out to dem

"Whats been eating you so bad?
en who's been tramping on your tongue
dat yous must shout so loud?"

De moegoes go one way

"Hey lange why's you not in school today?"

I get a vicious look dat make me back away
Dees kids dees little runts
I tell you –
were making war on want

Dey were shouting wid one voice
No more bad education
No more bad legislation
Wid dere fist in de air dey shouted FREEDOM

Some teachers try to tell em
"mustn't make trouble
is not too late to negotiate"
children erupt close de gates
en lock em out

Dose kids were not going to be given the run about

I said to myself kap it uit en go
I got to merge wid de mugus en disappear

Den de stones rain from de sky
doof duff boof
all over de blerry show
de police charge de cheering kids
en den I hear de guns

WOOM – WOOM – WARRA – WARRA

All over de blerry show
en children dead en children scream
en hell break loose from dis horrible scene

Kids get kwaai
wid bricks en sticks
dey jus let wip

Dey burn de cars en take a bus
en drive it reg deur de barricades

I did get carried away dat day
en help em do dis ting
we didrn't run from guns
Police shit demselves dat day
en call for reinforcements

Dey fought de cops burnt liquor shops
shouting "Drink don't make you think"

But I did liberate a bottle or two
to celebrate our victory

Cause I tell you right now jus how I feel
TODAY I'M A RESPECTABLE SKOLLIE

TWO TIME FREE TIME

And the band played on
while the banners danced
among the moving crowds

The music went by
with the razzmatazz
and a joint to keep you high

Moving and swinging
in time to a booming string bass
and the banging of two metal spoons

Today is freedom day
when all your dreams come true

Not you and you, not even the President
can tell me what to do
Today the law got his arm in a sling
so sing Bra sing with a voice of freedom

This our day to go
to make the mind blow
walk tall
while the music called the tune

The music played without no score
without no notes or nothing

Tunes from now and how we lived
and how we asked for more

Stick tapping time
on a black tarred road
cracked voices croon
melodies of love

THIS IS HOLLYWOOD TIME

Romance and Glitter
what's the use of feeling bitter

Voices trying to sing away the blues
today and yesterday and before
when they were buggered by the law

The bugaboo man
with a big white face
teaching you to know your place

Bodies prancing dancing conversating
we were in the mood for celebrating

Today I'm the outjie in the stuk
with me coloured top hat
and bright tail coat

Play that tune
with a two four six
and let the body
do the tricks

take a deep draw
and hold it down
this is the best dagga
you'll find in town

Dance boogie dance
the nights nog young

Dance round the town
while the whitemen watch

Jump up and down
and throw your stick
you're the Kapilaan the clown
just wave your prick

The night wears on
the booze is gone

Day-break is near
and the light of reality
will bring new fears

The knees feel weak
the head in a spin
the dagga was good
and so was the gin

Don't let tomorrow
sneak up on me
this is THE TIME
for a man like me

But tomorrow is coming
is coming you'll see
there'll be more than
one day for us to be free

DAGGA DREAMS

So to see
if only it could be
like heaven with shining motors
gliding through black holes
and shining souls with a golden halo

So to see
if only it could be
with the razzmatazz running fast and loose
bending to the buckling sound
of angel Gabriel blowing his cool horn
to the sounds of heavenly bliss

So to see
if only it could be
I the boss the big shot for all to see
with servants waiting graciously on me
while I wave them to and fro
with a flick of the finger

So to be
If only my voice
cooled the throbbing crowd
who cooed in ecstasy

But dreams dissolve back to reality
where sounds confront my heavenly bliss
back back back there you black bastard
Can't you read?
This entrance is for Whites only

KWELA

Heart beat heavy with the throb
plays heavy with the head
while the drummer drums drums

Demanding dance demanding frenzy
faster and faster into a feverish pitch
faster and faster with no control

Let my soul burn let it yearn
let it learn there's no reason
to excavate the dead dreams of childbirth

No reason to take the drums and make it talk
saying words no wise man would have dreamt
A communion of hand against a dead skin

We broken with tradition taken the drum
the heartbeat of the world
and allowed it to run its own rhythm

Turning people high for the sake of high
wise men say your words so change will come
say it say it say it

Then by and by we will fly into safety
but words are from the earth and the wise men
are silent waiting and knowing

That the voice that starts the drum
that starts the sound and plays for pay
is not his peoples way

The drummer drums drums
working his way with the beat rolling his sticks
in an ecstasy of the dance

Devil man dance and move the air
its all happening where it happened before
and wise men nod and move away

Turn and turning about he moves to the left
arm out and turn man possessed obsessed
possessed with success to turn and turn about

Hysterical and high he flies out to die
leaving the world of houses that houses images
and death and dance drowns victims dancing hard

into the ground – the ground – the ground

BREAKING TIME

INKABA

Our nerves stretch out
radiating pain
trying to touch the history of the past

Hope makes the heartbeat pump fast
pulse quickens as the nerves connect
and the feet move to a new dance

The shrift waters break
and ooze through the grief stricken eyes
giving birth to a new vision

Covered in the veil of mucus
dragging our cord of conviction
we confront the virile father of our destruction

Bathed in sunlight streaming through bullet holes
we wash away the mucus of revolution
and break bread for the first supper

But who will bury birth and destruction
and eat the father's force and heritage
in the sun-flooded fields of freedom – upon the
ocean of forgiveness who marry the mother of mercy

So together in the treasured embers
of a new beginning in new dreams
and new dimensions – we will be joined together

DEATH IN EXILE
Tribute to Johnny Dyani

The strains of being torn from the land of birth
face calm – fingers itching to touch the tension

To pluck from his memory the joys of his native earth
as he cut through the tension with a scythe curved bow

Reaping new sounds from past memories
while the beat of the earth was still in his brain

The voice of a mother's memory opened his mouth
as he sang the sounds of Africa

Warming white hearts trapped in an iced cold culture
raising the old ancestors and giving them a voice

For us he brought back memories weaving the sound
twanging sobbing sounds reverberating in our minds
for us he recreated home

His nimble fingers racing you along moving you
first this way then that way then stopping . . . . . .

Holding you in mid air before moving you on
for another dance

As he curved his finger to pluck the snapping string
the tension between life and death disappeared

The sound of his death reverberated in our minds
in silence we wait in anticipation
only to hear an echo of the last recorded sounds

Creating an emptiness in our hearts and minds
but not in our memories

AHMED TIMOL

The rain washes away the guilt
no trace of blood on the pavement below
only lies point towards the truth

They have translated injustice into justice
mocking the concept of truth and honour
their crooked minds have been arrested by greed

He was pushed from the buildings of Babylon
heavy against the hard cold ground he lies
They have translated murder into suicide

Words catching in the crop of his throat
teeth trapping sound – tongue tasting blood
brutalised by fat-bellied bullnecked baboons

Eyes bury themselves into the soft dark flesh
pitiless – cold – creeping into the crying mind
these white abominations have no feelings for pain

Flies flitting around Vorster square
living off dirt and sweet lies of injustice
with the occasional morsel of dead man's meat

They wanted names – names of troublemakers
beaten and mauled brain raw with pain – no mercy
only the murderous voices of his translators

TALK AND TELL – TALK AND GIVE THE NAMES
THIS IS NO GAME – TALK OR YOU DIE –
OR CAN YOU FLY?
his pain was high but his mouth refused to move

The translators of death lifted his broken body
towards the altar of an open window
a sacrifice of blood to the pavement below

Silence ended his short life
but how do we resurrect the pieces of his broken body
while murderers tell white lies to defend injustice

POET OF THE PEOPLE
(Benjamen Moloise)

He stood silently reflecting his dreams
in a nightmare reality

Wooden boards covering the drop of death
eyes struggling to meet the sky

Body too heavy to dance into a new dimension
thought spilling out towards the crowds

As they echoed his words forged by frustration
forged in heat of anger sharp as a razors edge

They were chanting their words those words
which were his words
heavy with the hurt of his peoples pain

He spat words in the face of the master race
staring into the mocking eyes of death

Head held high arms tied so he could write no more
obey the law and respect oppression – their words
as they dropped the noose around his neck

Sounds of singing in the lonely corridors of death row

THE THUD –

Heavy with the hurt of the body and brain
silently we stand on the verge of pain
waiting for the long drop of death

Waiting to receive his thoughts his voice his pain

BENJAMEN . . . .

We will cut the rope that burnt your neck
and silenced your voice there is no death for you –
only a long rest before the revolution

X MARKS THE SPOT
Tribute to Dulcie September

There is no answer to the question of death,
under the curfew of silence.
Deep – hearted shadow of broken passions
I grieve for you.
For I remember us standing in front of the
doorway of desolation –
exalted and eager for change
we picked up the gauntlet –
and you answered the challenge of oppression.

Under the silent wind of wisdom
Under a mournful memory
Under the mist of suppression
There is no answer to the question of death.

No answer to the question of death,
as you felt the reverberation of revolt.
Lovers were lost in the solitude of prison
but faith anchored you to the reservoir of change,
as deep affection overflowed –
stirring the strings of liberation
to play a tune of revelation.
But still there is no answer to the question of
death

No answer to the question of death only rage –
evoking the cold winter
when trees stood naked of their leaves,
against the dark clouds of fear.
No answer to this black and white dream –
shot in vivid colour
when the Paris police came to view
the murder scene .

ATHLONE

We walk –
we walk –
we walk in the wake of a dream
that flirts with death

No more
does the ground
dance to the sound of our feet
today it claps with anger

We march –
we march –
we march against the white mocking mind
in the making of a new destiny

Fear cries for loss
a new memory in the making
a new time for breaking the barricades
barb with bankers trying to bamboozle us

Banners waving on the dusty roads
daring to depict a new time
defiant voices of the dawn
ring with the rhythm of a new chant
drawing its energy from the old ancestors

Our humming is drowned
by the harsh haunting sounds
of the Hippo high with death

Hard cold grey
steel coffins
wheeling its way
towards the crowds

Camouflaged –
in the British bought tradition
camouflaged –
grey on the cold black streets

But what can camouflage
the stench of cordite
the helpless screams
corpses left on a black tarred road

The smell of petrol
bitter sweet from broken bottles
burn with broken people

Fingers twitch and clutch
twitch and clutch searching for something to throw
the twitching dies
as the clutch holds hope for freedom
It is a scene for making martyrs
in the grey exhaust of a clouded city

we walk
and the roads are wet
wet –
wet –
wet with blood wet with tears
for our brothers and sisters

we stagger –
we stagger our feet heavy
with the weight of our dead

Our minds –
heavy with misery but we keep going
we will not kneel nor will we bow

Our heads are held high
our shaking fist point to the sky

We know –
we know how they died
not helpless not aimless
not gods forgotten children
shot in the dark of night

But children smiling in the sunlight
marching in the daylight of liberation
full of the joys of life

As we walk
as we walk
as we walk in the wake of a dream
that flirts with death

LIFE SPREAD

Let sounds seduce the silence
making music between the spaces

Making tunes and tempting the solid
to melt and merge into the music

Voices unconscious float beyond the brain
to cup and drain the grains of twinkling stars

Away from the weight of worry we splice the dream
and join it to the reel immense in perversity

This moment muslined for a marriage
stood in the doorway waiting

Crowned with a circle of gnats
and decked in butterfly dreams

The dead tree welcomes me
barkless bleached against the green ivy

Grey minded against the green
wrapped in original sound

Looking for words that spiral
into a composition of nothingness

Hallucinations heal the homesick
plucked by the fingered sounds of words

Pointing to the original sounds of lovers
whose bodies understood each other

Let starlings with their yellow beaked sounds
pick the remnants of our minds

So that the avarice will be carried away
on the whirring wings of a dream

NEW TIME

Breaking through the shackled mind
      anointing the head
      with words of fire

Breaking through the vision of blackness
      letting stars twinkle
      in the tormented mind

Breaking through the unpurged nakedness of truth
      nourished by the tears of love
      body burst through the ground

      A black flower in the spring

Breaking through the waters of the womb
      so that sound slips gently through
      in its first cry for freedom

The baby is kicking and breaking new ground
Bury the umbilical cord wrapped in newspaper
to hide all signs of birth
but the baby lingers in the safety of the womb

      Child swaddled in education
      cannot fly from gravitation

Sing songs of birthright sing songs of freedom

      anvil hammered voice of steel
      from our new black Smith

How can I describe the necklace of black
burning around your neck

      the pot of gold
      at the end of the rainbow

The hole you dug that was also your grave

      This scribe has no pen
      she pricks her finger
      and writes with blood

She has no style only her throbbing heartbeat
as it pumps new patterns onto paper

The blood of crucifixion
anointing the head
new sounds – with words of freedom

DEATH OF MY FATHER

On awakening I found the scaffold
of self destruction waiting for me

It filled my body with the smell of decay
beckoning me with the arms of a lost lover

They say the lens does not lie
then the light must play tricks with the human eye

I saw benediction touch the breath of extinction
there on my pillow sculpture in nostalgia

was the the head of my father
the arteries of my head throbbed

Heartbeat pounded my brain – it was not constant
it was a wild spider making a mad web

The beats were shifting together
coming closer and closer together until

the beats all rolled into one – one bang that
shattered reality – this was my benediction

I was in the silent centre of the hurricane
transparent – I was the aboriginal anaesthetised

No heartbeat no horror hovered over me
in the emptiness – there was no point of action

I was beyond reproach and indifferent to sorrow
the smell of decay was the sweet joy of transience

The cranium craved for thought – for recognition
I felt myself drawn sucked into the swirl

whirling round into the emotion of tension and fear
my body heaved under each sob of death's empty echo

making everything futile empty and hollow
I hungered for the nourishment of my father's flesh

I was the beggarman with expectations for more
the lost sperm of creation divided from its origin

Commemorate the broken mosaics mirror
haemorrhaging as John Doe who does not know me now

EXILE

WHISPERS OF WHY

Ask me
how the moon makes the ocean rise
through a dark black sky

Ask me
how a non existent star twinkles
many many light years away

Ask me
whether I dream in the sky of illusions
or have I imagined myself into being

Ask me
why my mind is sticky and needs sweet love
while I sip a sublimate for comfort

Ask me
what this knife is that cuts through life
while time is always my challenger

Ask me
for in my fantasies I have become lost
and need questions for new assumptions

Ask me why
I conspire with the granite sky
so that it will merge with my granite mind

Unborn I wish to murder this wormwood of reality
with every afflicted word I speak

and they need a sacrifice for their existence
to give purpose for living they want my death

Tell me why
they moulded me in a furnace white with hate
when their laws doubt my very existence

Gently you touch me, fingers against a brown body
supporting the tortured remnants of sanity

MOURNING LETTERS

Gaoled mind hoping for an eternal land
how many nights do I lie awake

Worried with a troubled mind
disturbing myself with delirious talk

Listening to the wild wind lying in wait
and seeing dark distortions of myself

Inside my soul is bitter and there is no peace
lamentations for the dead is not enough

The howl is the heartbeat forcing blood to flow
it is hot and beats inside the brain

An echo of my childhood follows me
casting long shadows in my path

Death stalks steadily before me
why do I perform this futile rite of living

There is no need to sacrifice myself
too many martyrs have made that message

Who lives in hope lives in dreams
for ideals are filled with death

When we have murdered the history
and hung the fairy tale out in the open

The fetters will fall from our minds
I will dance on the dead letters of a dictionary

While my amputated hand will wave goodbye
to the words trapped inside my mind

INVOCATION

There is darkness
no light at the window
I work in solitude
sifting through syllables
to find woodwind sounds for words

Searching for the cipher
in a dream reality
I sleepwalk through sentences
tripping on spiderweb words
not fluent and flute sounding

My lips lick cold consonances
sweet lollypot iced creamed
in the scream of pain
Where are the sacred symbols
hidden in the runes?

How can I magic new meanings
with old indifferent idioms
I stalk the seeds of sounds
trying to find its descendants
in the cemetery of words

I am aware of inscriptions
on the reflecting tombstones
eye of isolation is watching me
with a glint of recognition
my mind mutters words

My hand cannot move it cannot script
how do I hide this ignorant hand
whose flippant fingers have failed
to capture the essence of sound
while my holy palms are silent

Inarticulate – the pen falls
from my nervous fingers
it plummets into space
sleep turns words into stars
which twinkle in the dark sky of the unknown

Echoing in dreams
the ghost world of the universe

OUTLANDER

The illusion that brought me to this land
lies like a shattered carcass of some
prehistoric being, waves wash away deception
reflecting only the night of dawn

It is the forest fire that crackles
to the cackle of the witches chant

It is the diamond of minds eye
sitting in the centre of my forehead.

It is a siren singing my seduction song
and moontide madness reflected on the water

All things come together in one crazy mind
liquid – in midst of chaos a memory plays tricks

In the dance of danger ordained by nostalgia
revelation has an afterglow of anger;
alcohol is the milk of mind madness
whitening the black symbolic skeletons,
to hide the archaeological dig of sadness.

Scream dreams of death
but where is deliverance ?
Come Mamma wipe my wounds,
while the rest cry onion tears –
over here very few follow funerals.

But who will bury me
in the clay soil of a cold country,
to nourish the rose petals skins,
while our fingers sticky with the sap
of the Protea touch the sharp pricks
called petals.

Lay the bloom of remembrances
upon this living grave

tell how you wiped away my pain
and pieced me together
while the sun hides behind the clouds
ashamed of my escape.

I marched towards the massacre of emotions
and met her by the shrine of forgetfulness –
we followed our dreams listening to its desires.

Then we heard the cry of the wind, the waves
washed around our thighs and lifted us high
before it brought us back to shore.

It is the grief of departure
from the land of occupation to the land
where occupation is the label of trade;
austerity, acquisition and hoarding
all reaching for the dreams of prosperity.

I had forgot what reality was like –
the leaking roof, the wind blowing through
the broken window pane.

Rain beating down on the corrugated iron roof
rattling my brain, with sharp staccato notes.
There is no romance in shitting in a cesspit
and waiting to hear the plop.

Looking over your shoulder to see
if you are being followed,
wondering who is going to be the next victim
stabbed to death.

These images came flooding back
as I searched for a house that was not there
the streets had disappeared into the mist of memory
all that remained was the rubble of oppression
our past had once again been obliterated

On this ground there once was – there once was

there once was even before the sea
we live on the surface of the past;
but what will be coming down to live on top of me?

Where is the romantic making dreams of love
from the scream sounds of anguish,
moulding the sounds into thought,
so that the butterfly mind could find its nectar
from the flowering sounds that music brought.

I hear the murmuring of the sea
the splashing sounds exploding against the rocks,
the lapping waves hungry for change.
I stand before the alter of images
galleried in the dark foundation of power,
and wait for the moment of freedom.

I wear the words of this culture
a suit that hangs loosely on the shoulders
of my mind, shoes shuffle around in my brain
making a dance for the blind.

I hammer my head against the words
demanding their submission –
they are slippery and silence my mouth.
Lips curl to colonial sounds and I show my teeth.
I gibber in front of the gibbet of words,
that hangs on the last encountered sounds.

I wet my blistered lips, the sea will not quench
my thirst, waves beat down on my resolute brain
I hear the splashing of the waterfall

The coming together of many drops of rain,
the river flows gently down among the banks
hidden by the ledge, the long tongue
slips snake like towards the waters edge.

Wetting the lips of words the river flows on
and the words disappear in whispers.

NOTES

Page v Khoi: a people named by the whites as Hottentots or Bushmen. They are also sometimes called Kung.

Page vi Mos: as you will, just do it.

Page 3 Oananua: mythical mother of the Khoi. Kanya: god of fire. Amatolas: these mountains are often mentioned in their legends. Mantis: an important Khoi god.

Page 8 Bid maar kinders, bid maar dis God se kruis wat ons moes dra: pray my children, pray it is gods cross that we carry Haikona: oh no, you cannot Xhosa: a language spoken by many people in the Cape Province, it is also said to be strongly influenced by the Khoi.

Page 10 Malau: person of mixed race. Majietas, Majietas, julle kan my nie voestaan nie: Spiv, Spiv, you cannot understand me.

Page 14 Hotnot: a shortened version of the word Hottentot, mostly used in a derogatory way to insult people.

Page 16 Kapilaan: someone who thinks he is a leader.

Page 21 Booi: boy Bosie: shortened version of the word Bushman, mostly used in a derogatory way to insult people.

Page 23 Kaffir: coming from the Arab word Kafir meaning infidel. In S.A. it is used in a derogatory way to define black people. Baas: boss Blerry: bloody. Foken: fucking.

Page 32 Heitsi-Eibib: Khoi god of the hunt. Hare's message: the Khoi gods told the Hare to tell the Khoi people that, as they die yet shall they live in the minds of their ancestral future. But the Hare ran so fast that he forgot the message, and told the Khoi people instead, that as they die, and dying perish, they shall die, utterly die.

Page 37 Autshumoa: leader of the Khoi, who were called the Strandloopers (beachcombers). The whites called him Herry the Hotnot, and he became their interpreter, he was also the uncle of Eva. Tusia Xgoa: one of the Khoi gods who is regarded as the father of all fathers.

Page 44 Guarra: a noise to denote the sound of guns. Darrah: father

Page 46 Kundalini: the snake power, a symbol of regeneration. In Indian teaching it lies coiled at the back of the spine. Deumba: snake dance, symbolic, life-generating, union of heaven and earth.

Page 51 Bankie: small bench. Joppa: a person known to both speakers.

Page 54 Modder: variation of moeder, mother. Ombaskofte: variation

of onbeskofte, rude. Pallie: friend, person known to us. Joep: wine
Shebeen: illegal drinking house
Page 56 Jy moes wakker wies: be awake, alert. Lighties (sometimes
spelt lieties): children. Pickanins: very small children. Stoep: veranda.
Moegoes: crazy people, idiots. Lange: tall one
Page 57 Kap it uit: run like hell. Kwaai: cross, very angry. Let wip:
go berserk. Reg deur: right through.
Page 58 Skollie: street-wise, gangster.
Page 60 Bugaboo man: monster, ogre. Outjie: hero, the star. Stuk:
scene. Dagga: marijuana. Nog: as well.
Page 63 Kwela: dance, or a type of music.
Page 67 Inkaba: umbilical cord.
Page 87 Protea: a flower found in S. Africa.

Some of the various clicks used by the Khoi

The tongue is pressed against curve of the hard palette producing a
sharp snapping sound. Dental click, used by placing the tongue behind
the upper incisors. Producing a soft 'tsk sound. The tongue remains
on the hard palette while the air vibrates at the sides. Tip of the tongue
is placed on the curve of the palette to produce a loud popping sound.